Labrador
Retrievers

ABDO
Publishing Company

A Buddy Book
by
Julie Murray

VISIT US AT
www.abdopub.com

Published by Buddy Books, an imprint of ABDO Publishing Company, 4940 Viking Drive, Suite 622, Edina, Minnesota 55435. Copyright © 2005 by Abdo Consulting Group, Inc. International copyrights reserved in all countries. No part of this book may be reproduced in any form without written permission from the publisher.

Printed in the United States.

Edited by: Christy DeVillier
Contributing Editors: Matt Ray, Michael P. Goecke
Graphic Design: Maria Hosley
Image Research: Deborah Coldiron
Photographs: American Kennel Club, Corel, Eyewire Inc., Photodisc

Library of Congress Cataloging-in-Publication Data

Murray, Julie, 1969-
    Labrador retrievers/Julie Murray.
        p. cm. — (Animal kingdom. Set II)
    Contents: The dog family — Labrador retrievers — What they're like — Coat and color — Size — Care — Feeding — Things they need — Puppies.
    ISBN 1-59197-324-4
        1. Labrador retrievers—Juvenile literature. [1. Labrador retriever. 2. Dogs.] I. Title.

SF429.L3M88 2003
636.752'7—dc21

                                                    2002043627

Contents

Dogs

At one time, dogs were wild like wolves. Nobody is sure when dogs became tame. Today, millions of people have pet dogs.

Wolves are related to dogs.

The American Kennel Club has named about 150 dog **breeds**. Every dog breed looks different. Some breeds, such as Great Danes, are big dogs. Other breeds, such as Chihuahuas, are small dogs. Every breed is special in its own way.

A Great Dane (left) and a Chihuahua (right).

Labrador Retrievers

Newfoundland is an island near Canada. Long ago, Newfoundland fishermen used dogs to help them pull in fishing nets. These Newfoundland dogs also **retrieved** fish from the icy water. Today's Labrador retrievers are related to Newfoundland dogs.

A Newfoundland dog

People in England used Labrador retrievers for bird hunting. These dogs were good at **retrieving** birds. Today, Labrador retrievers are popular pets in North America.

What They Look Like

Labrador retrievers are medium-sized dogs. Males grow to become as tall as two feet (one m). Male Labrador adults weigh between 65 and 80 pounds (29 and 36 kg). Females are smaller.

Labradors are strong and solid dogs. Their coat has two layers of hair. This hair protects them against the cold.

Labrador retrievers have a thick coat to keep them warm.

Labrador retrievers may be black, yellow, or chocolate brown. Most Labradors are one solid color. Some have a white spot on their chest.

Many Labrador retrievers are one solid color.

Labrador Retrievers As Pets

Labrador retrievers are friendly and trusting. They love to be around people. Labradors get along with children and other animals.

Labrador retrievers are great pets for children.

Labrador retrievers are sporting dogs. Sporting dogs enjoy exercise. Labrador retrievers are great pets for active people. Labradors also make good hunting dogs.

This Labrador retriever is learning to retrieve ducks.

Working Dogs

Labrador retrievers can learn to do special jobs. During World War II, they found land mines and traps. Today, Labradors can be trained as service dogs. Service dogs help people. Some pull wheelchairs. Some open and close doors for people. Service dogs guide blind people, too.

Grooming And Care

Grooming is important for all dogs. Brushing a dog's coat keeps it smooth and clean. Owners should brush their Labrador retrievers once a week.

Dogs need their nails clipped short. Cleaning a dog's teeth and ears is also important. Owners can ask a **veterinarian** how to do this.

Puppies and adult dogs need a veterinarian's care.

A **veterinarian** is a doctor for animals. Taking pets to a veterinarian helps them stay healthy.

15

Feeding And Exercise

All dogs need food and fresh water every day. Adult Labrador retrievers should be fed once a day. Try not to change your dog's food too often. A changing **diet** can lead to health problems.

Labrador retrievers enjoy being outside.

Retrieving sticks is good exercise for Labrador retrievers.

Labrador retrievers need space to run and play. They love swimming, running, and going on walks. Labradors enjoy **retrieving** games, too. Exercising every day helps them stay healthy.

Labrador retrievers enjoy swimming.

Puppies

Labrador retrievers commonly have **litters** of eight puppies. The puppies are born blind and deaf. They drink their mother's milk. Puppies will begin seeing and hearing at about two weeks old.

A Labrador retriever puppy

Puppies enjoy exploring.

Puppies should stay with their mothers for eight weeks. Labrador retrievers can live as long as 13 years.

Labrador retrievers are great pets.

Important Words

breed a special group of dogs. Dogs of the same breed look alike.

diet the food that a dog (or a person) normally eats.

groom to clean and care for.

litter the group of puppies born at one time.

retrieve to find and bring back.

veterinarian a doctor for animals. A short name for veterinarian is "vet."

Web Sites

To learn more about Labrador retrievers, visit ABDO Publishing Company on the World Wide Web. Web sites about Labrador retrievers are featured on our Book Links page. These links are routinely monitored and updated to provide the most current information available.

www.abdopub.com

Index